T0099240

Soul of Athens

A GUIDE TO 30 EXCEPTIONAL EXPERIENCES

WRITTEN BY ALEX KING
COVER PHOTO BY STEVEN BEIJER
BACK COVER PHOTO BY THEO MCINNES
ILLUSTRATED BY NONI NEZI

JONGLEZ PUBLISHING

travel guides

PHOTOGRAPHY: EFTYCHIA VLACHOU

"IT'S AN UNEXPECTED CITY,
A CITY THAT PROVOKES FANTASY
IN A WAY THAT NO OTHER
MAJOR EUROPEAN CITY DOES,
BECAUSE ATHENS IS *UNPREDICTABLE*."

NIKOS VATOPOULOS
JOURNALIST, PHOTOGRAPHER AND URBAN EXPLORER

WHAT YOU WON'T FIND
IN THIS GUIDE

- How to find the Acropolis (it's a massive rock, you can't miss it)
- The best selfie spots
- Tourist traps you'll find in every other guide book
- Athens' Michelin-starred restaurants (they're fantastic, check them out, but you don't need this book to find them)

WHAT YOU WILL FIND
IN THIS GUIDE

- The secrets of contemporary Greek cuisine
- A Nouvelle Vague drinking experience
- How to see two varieties of stars at once
- Athens' most agreeable goats
- Romantically charged shopping
- A chemistry set that produces the finest wine in Greece
- Fish that will send you to heaven
- A skaters' and art lovers' paradise
- Your ticket for the legendary Orient Express
- A goth club that will take you on a new wave timewarp
- The best Greek art collection that most Athenians don't know

This guide is not comprehensive — and it doesn't aspire to be. With a few very special exceptions, I've tried to share unique locations that you won't find anywhere else. If you want the top ten most popular spots, stick to TripAdvisor.

The approach I've taken with this book is to combine my own personal favourites — the places that made me fall in love with Athens — with the really hard-to-find, hidden gems, many of which I discovered only by following rabbit hole after rabbit hole in the process of writing and researching this book. Whittling down the list to just 30 special experiences has been tough — there's so much more of this amazing city I want to share with you — but any more would have been overwhelming. Save the rest for your next trip.

I've spent the past three years exploring all corners of Athens, usually on my bike — which few locals would advise. But in the past few months I've pushed myself to look harder, begged those far more knowledgeable than me to reveal their secrets, and have plunged deeper into Athens than ever before, all to distil that learning down into this book that you hold in your hands. So, read carefully — but don't be afraid to get lost: that's when the real Athenian adventures begin.

SYMBOLS USED IN
"SOUL OF ATHENS"

Free

Up to 40 euros

> 40 euros

Timewarp

Reservation
recommended

Soooo Athens!

Athens might just be the most misunderstood and underrated capital city in Europe. People tend to think of it as a living museum with a grubby and unremarkable modern city bolted on the side, which isn't worth their time. Most visitors shuttle back and forth between the ancient sites and tavernas in Plaka before heading off to their sun loungers on the islands. Of course, that is one side to Athens, and you can spend your whole stay locked in that trap, if you so choose. But you'll surely never touch the Soul of Athens that way.

Athena is a difficult one. She never makes things easy, but the challenges are far outweighed by the energy and opportunities that flow to all those who learn to love her. Find your way into the life of the (young) Athenians — who are intelligent, steeped in culture and experience, and always full of surprises — and you'll begin to understand why this city holds so many in awe. If recent years have proved anything, it's that the people of this city really know how to live, even in the darkest times.

Athens has been through more in the past decade than most cities go through in a hundred years. But then, the past century or so has been pretty eventful too. Athens sprang from little more than a village under the Acropolis in the mid-19th century to become one of the biggest cities in southern Europe. And most of what you see today appeared in the boom decades after World War Two. Expanding so fast, the growing pains are still visible: modern Athens is a chaotically unplanned sprawl that exploded out from the centre in an orgy of bulldozers, concrete and destruction of some of its most charming old buildings and neighbourhoods. It's not a conventionally beautiful city but its frenetic patchwork of geography and architecture does have its admirers. While development has swallowed up much of the city's green space, Athens more than compensates with mountains and, of course, the islands, just a stone's throw away.

The fight for space in Athens never ends. There's still an intense struggle going on over who the city is for. But, for now, unlike so many other cities around the world, no one side has claimed the ultimate victory. Even in the centre, artisans' workshops and frozen-in-time cafés often sit on the same street as the latest chic, third wave coffee shop. It's the most real city I know: an ever-changing time capsule, where the layers of history, empire, time, typography, architecture and art all overlap — and are plain to see.

In this book I've tried to strike a balance between the unique historical treasures which preserve the city's bonds to its heritage, and the latest creations of the bright young things who keep this city moving forward. Athens and its people have given me so much, have welcomed me in with open arms. This is, in part, my way of giving back: my love letter to Athens, which I hope makes you fall in love with her, too.

30 EXPERIENCES

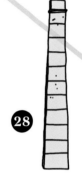

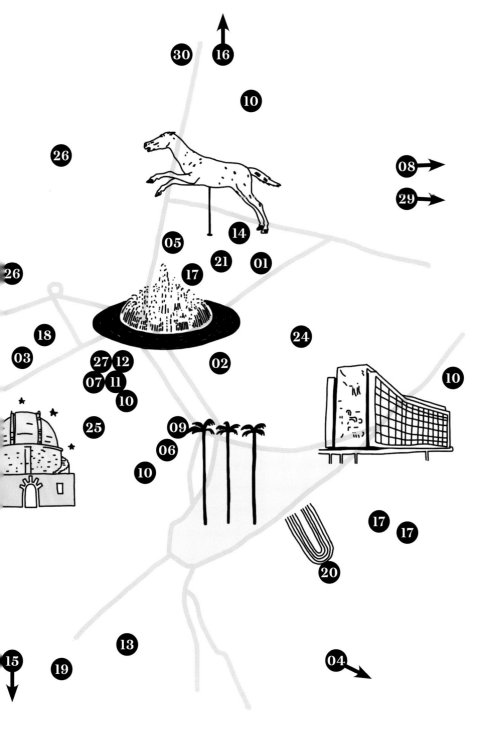

THE SCIENCE OF
GREAT WINE

For Stergios Tekeridis, the perfect glass is all a matter of science. Tanini Agapi Mou (Tanin, My Love) is equal parts wine bar, laboratory and urban greenhouse. Take your pick from the hand-selected list of over 120 Greek Protected Designation of Origin (PDO), Protected Geographical Indication (PGI) and local natural wines and you'll be served from what looks like a giant chemistry set. It is, in fact, a Coravin, which sucks the wine through a volumetric tube to ensure delivery into your glass at the perfect temperature and prevents air entering to degrade what remains in the bottle. The custom-built storage room behind the bar looks like a mainframe computer from seventies sci-fi, but is designed to keep bottles at a constant 15-17 °C and, ingeniously, at an angle so their corks stay wet. Cheeses and cold cuts from across Greece help catalyse a successful reaction from your taste buds. But if you want to be truly dazzled by the science of wine, ask for a lecture from Super Taninios. That's all I'll say...

 TANINI AGAPI MOU
IPPOKRATOUS 91
EXARCHEIA, 106 80

DAILY: 5pm – 1am
MON: closed

+30 211 115 0145

@tanini_agapi_mou
on Instagram

PHOTOGRAPHY: ANGELOS GIOTOPOULOS

02

WAKE UP IN
NEOCLASSICAL ATHENS

It's fair to say Athens doesn't sufficiently treasure its neoclassical architecture. Thanks to a range of factors, such as bureaucracy and restrictive planning laws, the city is dotted with palatial 19th century residences, slowly decaying and in need of repair. But Monsieur Didot shows what can be done when these incredible buildings are lovingly restored.

The boutique hotel was saved from ruin and given a literary identity that pays homage to Ambroise Firmin Didot, a French entrepreneur who brought his grandfather's typeface to Greece with a field press during the Greek War of Independence in 1821. He went on to set up a printing house nearby and the Didot font has been used extensively in Greek publishing ever since. In each of the one-of-a-kind rooms you can find immaculate design, exposed elements from the building's history and a great array of reading material. Steeped in literary tradition, it's a great place to stay if you need inspiration to pen your next masterpiece.

MONSIEUR DIDOT
SINA 48
KOLONAKI, 106 72

110-180€/night

+30 210 363 7625
+30 694 894 9185

monsieurdidot.com

03

SKATE AND CHILL IN
AN URBAN OASIS

Take a wrong turn in Kerameikos and you can easily stumble upon
a brothel or some very in-your-face drug use. But a skateboarding
oasis lies hidden behind tall metal gates on Leonidou Street.
Latraac is a skate bowl and experimental social space built by
Greek architect and skater Zachos Varfis, which has fast become
a mecca for skaters of all stripes — as well as artists, musicians and
ex-pats. There's nothing quite like it — in Greece or anywhere else
— where you can just as easily stumble upon avant-garde dance, as
far-out music nights or bowl contests for the core skate crew.

LATRAAC SKATE BOWL
LEONIDOU 63-65
KERAMEIKOS, 104 35

| TUE–SUN: 5pm – 1am | +30 213 045 3377 | latraac.com |

04

SWIM FREE OF
THE CITY

With Greece's enviable selection of islands just a short ferry's ride away, people often forget that Athens has its own beaches. Although many locals still dive from the rocks for a dip, it is probably best to avoid the water close to the boats in Piraeus harbour. The Athenian Riviera begins at Palaio Faliro and the coastline stretches for 60 kilometres, as far south as the magnificent Temple of Poseidon at the tip of Cape Sounion.

The prime beaches with their golden sands and crystal clear waters only really begin from Vouliagmeni onwards, where you have a range from the luxuriously equipped Astir Beach all the way to idyllic rocky coves such as Limanakia or Kape. Even the most distant are reachable in under two hours by bus or car from central Athens. End your day with a decadent fish dinner in Varkiza at NAOBB, a taverna attached to the local nautical club, where the tables spill out on to the beach.

You can also find even more great beaches north of Sounion, up to Porto Rafti, or around Schinias.

**VARIOUS LOCATIONS
SOUTH FROM PALAIO FALIRO**

PHOTOGRAPHY: MANOS CHATZIKONSTANTIS

BAR

Au revoir

05

GET DRUNK
LIKE GODARD

Au Revoir is an idiosyncratic drinking hole believed to be the oldest bar in Athens. As the name would suggest, it has a French atmosphere — but this is France as imagined by a Greek in an Athenian outdoor cinema in the 1950s, watching Nouvelle Vague movies such as François Truffaut's *Les Quatre Cents Coups* or Jean-Luc Godard's *À Bout de Souffle*.

Au Revoir was opened in March 1958 by brothers Theodoros and Lysandros Papatheodorou and it is still in the family. The France it seeks to imitate may never have existed, except on the silver screen, but a night at Au Revoir is always a memorable affair, with an artsy, international crowd who talk passionately long into the night.

 AU REVOIR
PATISSION 136
KYPSELI, 112 57

WED–SUN: 8:30pm – 2am   +30 210 823 0474

PHOTOGRAPHY: ORESTIS SEFEROGLOU

06

SCHOOL YOURSELF
IN GREEK
GASTRONOMY

If you want to immerse yourself in the world of Greek cuisine, head straight to Ergon House. The Ergon brand has grown from a deli opened by two brothers from Thessaloniki in 2011, to become a network of small, independent producers across Greece — and sold around the world.

Their modern take on the ancient agora (market) comes stocked with over 1,200 artisan products and boasts a bar, restaurant, greengrocer's, butcher's, fishmonger's, bakery, delicatessen and coffee roastery on site. It even has a 25-metre-high vertical garden which grows seasonal vegetables and herbs — all harvested by a resident abseiling gardener.

The cavernous atrium feels like a grand athenaeum of Greek gastronomy — but perhaps the correct metaphor is a foodie university, as devoted students can check into the chic hotel rooms upstairs and prepare their own culinary creations in the purpose-built kitchens. Wine seminars, cooking lessons and tasting sessions are also available, so you can educate yourself in the richness of Greece's culinary culture. Top marks are rewarded with cocktails on the rooftop, which is open to the public.

ERGON HOUSE
MITROPOLEOS 23
SYNTAGMA, 105 57

DAILY: 9am – midnight   +30 210 010 9090   house.ergonfoods.com

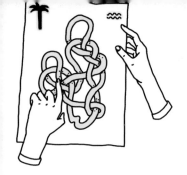

07

GET LOST IN AN
URBAN LABYRINTH

Exploring the old covered arcades, or stoas, which are hidden across Athens takes you into another world — and another time. The eerie, labyrinthine passageways, illuminated signage and vintage Greek typography feel like being inside a retro-futurist Balkan *Blade Runner*. The only way for outsiders to uncover the treasures of this city-within-a-city is to join Natassa Pappa, graphic designer and publisher of *Desired Landscapes* magazine, on one of her Athens Walkthrough guided walks.

The project grew out of Natassa's efforts to document the city's fading image, focusing on vernacular typography. She used this as a guide to re-energise paths through the commercial centre and encourage wandering in neglected corners of an urban fabric torn apart by crisis. With the help of Natassa's thought-provoking guidance, you'll discover bizarre architecture, craftspeople plying bygone trades and subterranean sections of the city's ancient walls.

 ATHENS WALKTHROUGH

MON–SAT: 10am – 4pm | Bookings upon request:
walks@desired-landscapes.com

ΔΕΛΤΑ
Η Δέλτα
της γειτονιάς

STAR
ρες

Ο φρεσκοκομμένος
καφές σας

ΠΡΟ-ΠΟ
ΛΟΤΤΟ
ΜΕ
COMPUTER

ΚΑΦΕΝΕ
το Στέκι

ΔΩΡΑ
ΜΠΙΖΟΥΤΑ

ΦΩΤΟΑΝΤΙΓΡΑΦΑ

MANN

ώρα για
COOPER

Ανθη
φυτα

Ραδι

ΗΛΕΚΤΡΙΚΑ

ΓΡΑΦΑΙ

σεις
τω
ΕΝΤΙΚΙΟΥΡ

ΛΟΡΙΦΕΡ
28.22.332

- NATASSA PAPPA -

DESIGNER AND PUBLISHER OF *DESIRED LANDSCAPES* MAGAZINE

"The crisis gives you balls" was the stand-out quote from my first interview with Natassa, way back when I first arrived in Athens. And it sums up Natassa's approach to life and work; she is a creative powerhouse, involved in so many of the most original projects to come out of Athens in recent years.

When did design and the city come together for you?
I was always interested in the city, without actually realising this was my theme. My BA thesis was a magazine intended to be left in public places. People could pick up, comment, change the content and rip off pages. It was a great collaboration with Danai Dragonea and contributing journalists, artists

and photographers. It was my first experiment with merging public space and graphic design.

How has Athens inspired you?
When I moved back from studying in Holland, I felt like Athens was a very exciting

PHOTOGRAPHY: NATASSA PAPPA

playground to explore. But my obsession with order couldn't really bear the chaos of the city, so I thought of documenting my urban experiences. I started drawing personal maps, marking my memories of the city. But when I went into the old arcades, I realised there was a need to make this mapping public, which became the *Into Stoas* project.

How's the design scene in Athens?
It's intriguing and now exports design, as most studios have clients abroad. Design is much more integrated in our everyday surroundings. The best include Bend, G Design Studio, MNP, Vasilis Marmatakis, Yannis Karlopoulos & Associates, and also the animators Odd Bleat. As a design educator, I see a new generation developing and I'm very optimistic about their future projects.

What is *Desired Landscapes*?
I have been researching representations of the urban experience for years. The success of my *Into Stoas* project allowed me to meet people from around the world, who each had stories to share: similar buildings in their own countries or places in other cities which conjured the same feelings. I began to explore the contrasts and patterns with others who were analysing the city: architects, journalists and photographers. *Desired Landscapes* is a compendium of different perspectives, alternative ways to explore cities and learn about new places, without departing the classical genre of the city guide.

How can design unlock the city?
My strategy is never give out everything. You have to create a mystery. It's like an invitation to curiosity. You have to give enough to create a trigger but leave the rest to the reader. Proscribing everything produces stress. You must create a balance between getting lost and feeling lost.

Share a special corner of Athens
Stoa Anatolis makes me feel at home. There are old printer's workshops in the basement, a cafe surrounded by plants on the ground floor, studios on the balconies and you can have an urban picnic when the roof is unlocked.

AN ART LOVER'S
HIDEAWAY

Inside this serene, walled enclave, it's easy to forget where you are, or even which century you're in. Part ethnographic museum, part avant-garde gallery, Vorres Museum is a little-known retreat from the cacophony of the city, that presents art, artefacts and ephemera from two-and-a-half millennia of Greek history side by side.

The seeds of this eclectic museum were sown when Ian Vorres returned to Greece from Canada in 1964. Dismayed by the 'destruction' he saw during a period of frenetic post-WWII urbanisation, Vorres vowed to save as much of Greece's disappearing pre-industrial cultural wealth as he could. He renovated a 19th century house and stables in the village of Paiania to house his growing bounty of treasures, to which he later added one of the finest collections of Greek contemporary art. You could easily spend a day in Vorres' timeless sanctuary, as the passage of the hours and years begins to lose all meaning.

 VORRES MUSEUM
PARODOS DIADOCHOU KONSTANTINOU 1
PAIANIA, 190 02

SAT–SUN: 10am – 2pm
WEEKDAYS by appointment
CAFÉ/BAR: TUE+THU 4pm – 1am

+30 210 6642520
+30 210 6644771

vorresmuseum.gr

THE STORE THAT SELLS
ANCIENT GREEK SANDALS

Ancient Greek Sandals is a brand with one foot — no pun intended — in the heritage and aesthetics of the ancient world and the other placed firmly in the contemporary fashion scene. Created by Christina Martini and Nikolas Minoglou, like many of the best Athenian brands today, it brings together old and new in a way that's chic yet playful.

The sandals themselves are handmade by skilled local craftspeople who use traditional techniques honed over centuries, and chemical-free, natural tan leather, which ages beautifully with wear and the passage of time. Their smart concept store near Syntagma is decorated with fabrics, plants and Aegean blue ceramic tiles, typical of Greek hotels from the sixties and seventies — creating a fusion of homey and holiday vibes. Alongside the sandals, they offer a curated range of Greek lifestyle products, such as olive oil, soap, candles and pottery.

 ANCIENT GREEK SANDALS
KOLOKOTRONI 1
SYNTAGMA, 105 62

MON–WED–SAT: 10am – 6pm TUE–THU–FRI: 10am – 8pm	+30 210 323 0938	ancient-greek-sandals.com

10

GIVE YOURSELF A
CAFFEINE CULTURE HIT

Coffee is something of a religion in Athens. It's a source of energy, a social lubricant and, in icy *freddo* form, also a means to survive some searing temperatures during summer. In recent years, owners and baristas have raised the bar with a new wave of coffee meccas that offer not just the finest hot and cold brews, but remarkable design, healthy and tasty bites, and ambiences that beg you to stay all day. Here are four of the best.

LOT 51

This strikingly bold neon-lit space in Ilisia looks like the coffee shop that American pop artist Ed Ruscha would have created if he had moved to Malibu and tried his hand at being a barista. The neon glow is complemented by a tropical beach atmosphere. You can start your day with sweet or savoury brunch and end it with refreshing cocktails. Beans are supplied by Athens' celebrated Area 51 Coffee Roasters, co-founded by Lot 51's owner, Konstantinos.

LOT 51
PAPADIAMANTOPOULOU 24B
ILISIA, 115 28

MON–FRI: 7:30am – 2am   +30 693 733 7066
SAT: 8am – 4am
SUN: 9am – 2am

ANANA

Housed in one of the finest restored Bauhaus buildings in Athens, dating from 1936, Anana is one of the most heavenly spaces to catch up over a brew. The airy space spills out into an old courtyard, is lined with plants and always attracts a diverse crowd. Anana prides itself in sourcing and roasting speciality single-origin beans from small producers. Its selection of vegan and vegetarian plates and vegan sweets is unsurpassed anywhere else in Athens.

ANANA
PRAXITELOUS 33
MONASTIRAKI, 105 60

MON–FRI: 8am – 9pm
SAT: 8:30am – 8pm
SUN: 10am – 8pm

+30 21 1115 1788

THIRD PLACE

Third Place's many eye-catching pieces of design make you feel like you're in a concept store for the coffee shop of the future. But Third Place is about far more than style, as their impressive range of coffees goes to show. Borrowing its name from sociologist Ray Oldenburg, who designated the 'Third Place' as the community space outside the home and the workplace, the shop more than delivers on this promise.

KICK

The latest arrival to the rapidly evolving neighbourhood of Kypseli is Kick, a coffee shop meets concept store and creative hub, from the creators of the Indiego clothing brand. Alongside their own wares, you can check out pieces from other small Greek skate and lifestyle brands, enjoy craft beer on tap and snack on edible delights from Eri Bakes Vegan and Cookie Dude.

 THIRD PLACE
APOLLONOS 23B
SYNTAGMA, 105 57

KICK
SPORADON 26
KYPSELI, 113 61

MON-FRI: 9am – 9pm +30 21 1182 4014
SAT: 10am – 9pm
SUN: closed in summer

MON-FRI: 8am – 10pm +30 21 1119 0369
SAT: 9am – 10pm
SUN: 10am – 9pm

11

PEDAL WITH
THE PUNKS

Most Greeks will tell you that nobody is crazy enough to cycle in Athens: the heat, the hills and the erratic drivers are just too off-putting. But take an evening stroll through the Psyrri neighbourhood, a warren of winding Ottoman streets packed with small artisans' workshops, and you'll find an eclectic bunch of bikers sipping beers on Melanthiou Street — a once-derelict spot now alive with colour. Vicious Cycles Athens and its next-door drinking hole, the Handlebar, have become the centre for Athens' alternative cycling community. Buzzing on summer nights, Melanthiou is regularly locked down for alleycat races, street parties and punk gigs, which nourish the emerging urban cycling scene.

 **VICIOUS CYCLES ATHENS
AND THE HANDLEBAR
8 MELANTHIOU
PSYRRI, 105 54**

MON–SAT: Noon – 1am

PHOTOGRAPHY: THEO MCINNES, ANGELOS GIOTOPOULOS (TOP)

12

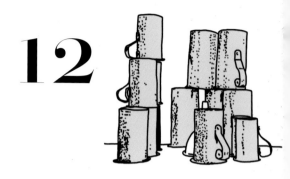

THE TAVERNA
THAT DOESN'T
WANT TO BE FOUND

Don't be tempted to snack on the technicolour herbs and spices on Evripidou street or other edible delights displayed around the Varvakios Central Market. Instead, keep your appetite intact and get lunch at central Athens' oldest and most idiosyncratic taverna, Diporto, founded in 1875. Down a trap-door beneath a dilapidated building opposite the vegetable market, you'll find Dimitris, the white-haired master of ceremonies holding court from a tiny open kitchen.

With no menu, you take whatever worker's fare has been prepared each day. A typical spread could be freshly caught fish of the day, chickpeas, potatoes with courgette and crusty bread, washed down with white Moschofilero wine, poured from the enormous wooden barrels stacked along one side of the cellar. This is definitely no-frills dining and if you ask for a knife, you'll be told, "If you want a knife go to (the well-heeled neighbourhood) Kolonaki."

Go early or off-season and you'll catch Diporto full of locals only.

 DIPORTO
9 SOKRATOUS
OMONOIA, 105 52

MON-SAT: 8am - 7pm

PHOTOGRAPHY: DIMITRIS VLAIKOS

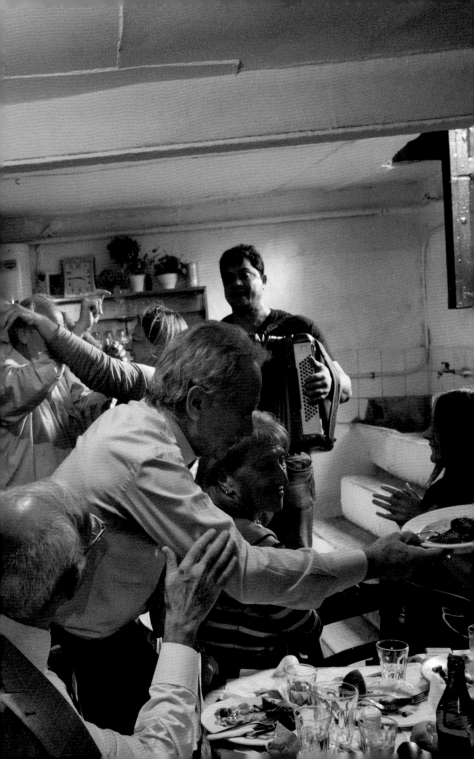

13

GET A
HERBAL EDUCATION

Cooking with herbs is a staple of the Mediterranean tradition. Inside the sublime store and laboratory of Daphnis and Chloe in Neos Kosmos, you'll find the very finest herbs and spices, sourced from small, natural producers across Greece. The country's varied geography plays host to an incredible biodiversity, with many isolated parts that have unique climatic conditions, making for some of the best herbs in the world.

Each product is painstakingly researched and the whole process, from harvesting to treatment and packaging, is developed by founder Evangelia Koutsovoulou to ensure every batch conveys the feeling of being freshly picked from the islands or the mountainside. Drop by for a chat at the tasting table, where you'll learn about the flavours and health benefits of each herb, so you can make them sing in your own cooking — whether you grab wild thyme flowers, Aegean Isle oregano or the Ancients' favourite, pennyroyal mint.

 DAPHNIS AND CHLOE
MANDROKLEOUS 19
NEOS KOSMOS, 11744

MON–FRI: Noon–5pm | +30 210 924 1012 | daphnisandchloe.com

HERBS

Daphnis and Chloe founder Evangelia Koutsovoulou selects the staple herbs of Greek gastronomy and explains their health and flavour benefits.

YOUR GUIDE TO
GREECE'S ESSENTIAL HERBS

GREEK MOUNTAIN TEA

This delicate tea which grows at altitudes of over 900 metres is the national herbal tea. Rich in precious antioxidants and naturally caffeine-free, it's one of the best infusions for sipping all day long, either hot or chilled. Little known elsewhere, it's omnipresent in Greek kitchens.

GREEK OREGANO

Definitely the most well-used spice in our cuisine and for good reason; Greece grows some of the best oregano in the Mediterranean. There are several different varieties but the whole bunches of mountain oregano are absolute classics.

WILD THYME FLOWERS

These come from shrubs that blossom by the sea around May. They're totally different to your local grocer's thyme and quite hard to find, due to the laborious harvesting process. Crumble a couple of flowers over grilled zucchini, add olive oil and lemon, and you have the ultimate Greek seasoning.

DITTANY FROM CRETE

Dittany is an endemic plant of Crete, meaning that it grows only there. According to local legend, this is the herb of love — so hard to harvest that one had to be deeply in love to endure the process. It makes a sophisticated herbal tea with characteristic bitter notes.

BAY LEAVES

Essential across the Mediterranean, bay leaves play a special role in Greek cuisine. Many people think they are pointless, but that's because they've never tried any good ones! Here, it's unthinkable to cook a stew or a lentil soup without them. They're also a key ingredient for preserving figs.

14

FOOD SHOP
LAIK-I LOCAL

Unlike many other European cities, where overpriced farmer's markets are a belated attempt to roll back the dominance of the supermarket giants, Greeks never lost connection with where their food comes from. The *laiki agora* or people's market is a staple of life here — just as it always has been.

Every week, you can peruse the latest seasonal produce — vegetables, fish, meat, dairy and sometimes clothing and more — from farms around Athens and across Greece at incredibly reasonable prices. One of the largest and most well-established laikis is on Kallidromiou Street in Exarcheia every Saturday morning. It's as much a social experience as it is a shopping experience for locals, with live music played, coffees consumed, issues of the day discussed and even romances ignited.

But, wherever you're staying, there will be a *laiki* a few streets away — just ask a local when and where.

LAIKI AGORA
KALLIDROMIOU
EXARCHEIA, 114 73

SAT: 7am – 3pm

PHOTOGRAPHY: ANGELOS GIOTOPOULOS

SAILING CLUB N.O.78
MARINA DELTA
KALLITHEA, 176 74

Lessons start between 9am and 11am
and last six to eight hours. Daily, May
through October.

+30 697 540 1075

no78.gr

15

TAKE TO THE
WAVES UNDER ATHENA'S GAZE

There are few vessels that still ply the waves with such a rich backstory as *Athena*. This traditional wooden sailing yacht was commissioned by the late Kostas Gouzelis, a revered architect, documentary maker and passionate chronicler of the Aegean sea and the people who live on its waters and along its shores.

Athena was built at Kanonis shipyard in Aegina and completed in 2011, using traditional Greek techniques, such as its Symian timber hull and two-masted bratsera rigging, but it sports Chinese junk sails. This was Gouzelis' way of expressing his love for travel, adventure and cultures of the world: like dragon wings growing out of Poseidon's back, he once said. Before you set sail, make sure to watch *Athena Ex Nihilo*, a documentary that celebrates *Athena's* construction and traditional Greek shipbuilding.

Sailing lessons aboard *Athena* explore the Saronic Gulf, take up to eight people and are tailored to the skill level of each group. You depart from Marina Delta in Kallithea, which is as close to the centre of Athens as you can get by sea and right in front of the Stavros Niarchos Foundation Cultural Centre. Your skipper will be Stelios Noutsos, a member of the Hellenic Olympic Team and organiser of the Okeanida regatta of classic and contemporary wooden boats, one of Athens' most special autumn events.

16

BE KING
FOR A DAY

You might hear whispers about an abandoned royal palace in the hills surrounding Athens, where you can walk through the grounds and freely explore the slowly decaying buildings. They say there are luxury cars rusting in ruined garages, as if the former inhabitants had been forced to flee in a hurry. The stories might sound fantastical, but they're true: 35 kilometres outside Athens lies Tatoi Palace, the former Greek royal family's summer retreat.

Ever since King Constantine II was forced out of the country following the 1967 military coup, the palace and its grounds have lain abandoned. Plans to turn the palace into a museum never materialised and Tatoi remains a lost beauty, withering away in the depths of the forest. Today, you can explore the winery, garage, cemetery, stables, and its (now empty) swimming pool. It's a great place for a hike or a mountain bike ride along the many trails that criss-cross the sprawling grounds. A timeless antidote to the irrepressible hustle of Athens.

TATOI ROYAL PALACE
TATOIOU
ACHARNES, 136 72

17

WATCH STARS
UNDER THE STARS

As long as I live in Athens, I will never grow tired of watching old movies in the open air. Every summer you can watch a diverse programme that ranges from Italian neo-realist classics to vintage horror and the latest Hollywood blockbusters — all shown in their original language with Greek subtitles (some cinemas also have English subtitles for films in a third language). Cine Paris and Cine Thision pop up in all the guides, but venturing a few minutes away from the centre will reveal some true retro-cinema delights, where what's happening on the silver screen is just a sideshow to the main event.

The oldest, Aegli, inside the Zappeion Gardens, dates back to 1903, while Riviera in Exarcheia is a true picture palace, where you can watch the action unfolding on neighbours' balconies above the screen, too. Or, Cine Palas in Pangrati, where the art deco neon masterpiece evokes the golden age of cinema and has remained virtually unchanged since it opened its doors in 1925.

But my personal favourite is nearby Cine Oasis, where the screen is nestled amongst tall apartment buildings, but you'd never know because you're surrounded on all sides by a garden of jasmine and camellias, replicas of ancient statues and assorted kitsch film memorabilia. A magical experience.

RIVIERA	CINE PALAS	CINE OASIS
VALTETSIOU 46	IMITTOU 109	PRATINOU 7
EXARCHEIA, 106 81	PANGRATI, 116 33	PANGRATI, 116 34
+30 21 0384 4827	+30 21 0751 1868	+30 21 0724 4015

CINE RIVIERA

CINE OASIS

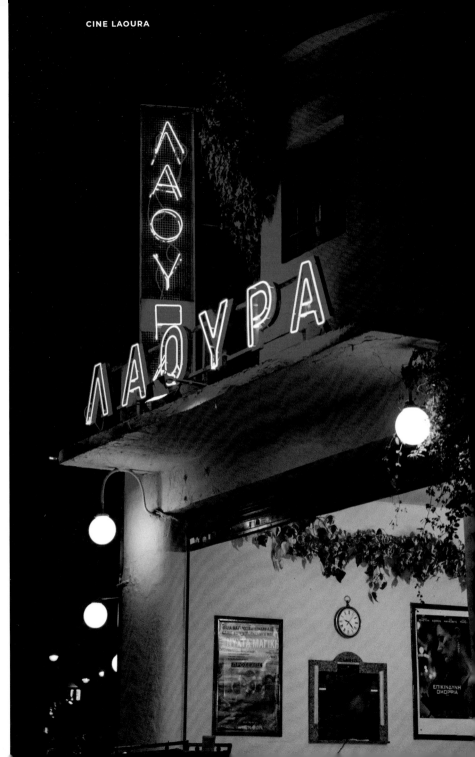

18

FIND YOUR
COMMUNITY

You often hear the ruckus from inside Communitism before you see it. Housed in a labyrinthine old mansion-cum-workshop, the building that houses this community-run art space looks like it could fall down at any minute. But while its guardians slowly restore the place from inside, it hosts some of the most wild and original events in Athens: from political discussions to art shows, Balkan brass band spectaculars and techno parties. It's a lottery what you'll stumble across on any given day but there are few places that embody the chaotic creativity of Athens better than Communitism.

 COMMUNITISM
KERAMIKOU 28
METAXOURGEIO, 104 36

Check website for event programme | communitism.space

PHOTOGRAPHY: THALIA GALANOPOULOU

PHOTOGRAPHY: KYRIAKOS BANOS/
ERGATIKI ALLILEGGYI ARCHIVE

FOTIS FOTINOGLOU & THODORIS KASSAVETIS

19

NEW SCHOOL
GREEK CUISINE

To the undiscerning eye, Fita might look like just another neighbourhood taverna. Yet this is anything but. The brainchild of Fotis Fotinoglou and Thodoris Kassavetis, Fita is all about simplicity, freshness and flavour. Each day starts with a trip to the market to pick up the best seasonal offerings from small farms and producers. Back in the kitchen, the menu takes a new shape each day, according to where the produce takes them.

Given the chef/owner duo's high-end pedigree, the down-to-earth dining experience comes as a surprise to some visitors. The location is out on a limb, next to the tram tracks in Neos Kosmos. But at Fita, even the most demanding customers leave satisfied. The honest food speaks for itself: Greek staples such as vlita or grilled sardines, served up without pretension but with impressive attention to detail, innovative flourishes and unexpected combinations. Fita is the finest embodiment of the very best of modern Athenian cuisine today.

 FITA
NTOURM 1
NEOS KOSMOS, 117 45

TUE-FRI: 7pm – Midnight
SAT: 2pm – Midnight
SUN: 2pm – 6pm

+30 211 414 8624

20

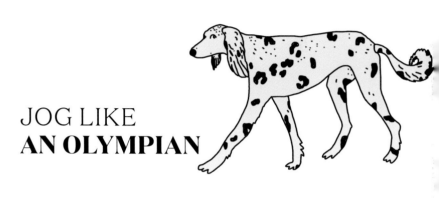

JOG LIKE
AN OLYMPIAN

Sure, you can pay the entrance fee for the Kallimarmaro, or Panathenaic Stadium, built to host the first modern Olympic Games in 1896 on a site home to athletic exploits since 330 BC. But locals enter the park that rings the stadium from the rear, to walk their dogs and jog with some spectacular views of this majestic white marble stadium. Climb further up into the trees of Ardittos Hill, to the west of the stadium, and you'll be rewarded with an even more impressive vista, that takes in the centre of Athens and the Acropolis.

KALLIMARMARO
ARCHIMIDOUS 16
PANGRATI, 116 36

Walk through the gates and through the courtyard,
then head up and to the left.

- LOST ATHINA -

YOUR TAXI TO THE ATHENS UNDERGROUND

Whether it's organising illegal alleycat races or street art shows in abandoned buildings, you'll never find Lost Athina too far away from the beating pulse of urban Athens. Filmmaker and photographer Angelos Giotopoulos heads up a Greek-Australian trio who have dedicated themselves to celebrating Athens' little-known facets and subcultures.

What convinced you to relocate from Melbourne to Athens?
Freedom. It's not as if we were caged in Melbourne, but once you have lived in Athens you truly understand the difference. There's a grittiness and a rawness that is in your face daily. Being a documentary photographer, I find stories around every corner, which satisfies my personal needs; but it's also just interesting to exist amongst it all.

INTERVIEW

What is Athens, to you?
Athens is a place where you can lose yourself with your eyes wide open.

What's unique about Athens' urban culture?
I believe it's on its own path. When you hit rock bottom the only way is up. The financial crisis gave people more reason to up their game, think outside the box and try to rattle people's idea about what we're actually going through. Underground culture blossomed because everyone became their own shadow to stay out of the light. They never stopped creating, it was just more low-key.

What is Lost Athina all about?
Lost Athina is about celebrating the city's raw soul. She makes it hard to survive but she also helps you along with plenty of opportunities. You just need to be tuned in to her unique frequency. We're trying to celebrate daily life here and remind people what is really going on.

An Athens must-see?
I will cheat that question and say the streets. You'll get to see much more than going to just one location.

Check out more urban stories on photography and film.
@LostAthina on Instagram.

21

GROW YOUR OWN
URBAN JUNGLE

From their chic store in Exarcheia, Kopria's owners, Ifigenia and Vassilis, are leading a campaign to turn Athens green — one house plant at a time. Kopria is the Greek word for "manure" but everything about their slick operation smells like roses. If picking up a plant on your travels isn't all that practical, the store also stocks a curated selection of handmade ceramics, Greek and international indie publications, tote bags and much more besides — you'll just have to pick your way through the mass of climbing plants, leaves and undergrowth to find them. The space is also an art gallery and hosts social gatherings and discussions on everything from art and sustainability to the urban environment. Their surreal Instagram account will keep you chuckling with plant-based visual gags, even after you've left Athens.

 KOPRIA
ERESOU 30
EXARCHEIA, 106 80

MON–FRI: 11am – 9pm	+30 211 113 2535	@kopriastore on Instagram
SAT: 11am – 7pm		
SUN: Closed		

PHOTOGRAPHY: KOPRIA

whatever makes you grow

kopria

22

A PRETTY PICTURE
BESIDE THE PORT

A small street in the old industrial area next to the mighty Piraeus port is the unlikely destination for an emerging international art hub. Paleo Wine Store started this new wave and serves up incredible dishes to accompany its impressive selection of wines, from inside a lovingly restored old warehouse building. It was joined by Rodeo Gallery, which relocated to Athens from Istanbul, and whose remarkable cavernous space sometimes risks overshadowing the world-class contemporary art shows hosted there. The latest arrivals have cemented Polidefkous street's new identity as a unique cultural destination: The Intermission art space and Carwan Gallery, which celebrates designers from the Near East region, Greece and beyond and which recently relocated here from Beirut, Lebanon.

PALEO WINE STORE	**RODEO GALLERY**	**CARWAN GALLERY**
POLIDEFKOUS 39	POLIDEFKOUS 41	POLIDEFKOUS 39
PIRAEUS 185 45	PIRAEUS 185 45	PIRAEUS 185 45
MON-SAT: 6:30pm - Midnight	WED-SAT: 2pm - 10pm	WED-SAT: 2pm - 8pm
+30 210 412 5204	+30 210 412 3977	+30 210 411 4536

23

WHERE FISH
MEETS FIRE

A meal at Dourabeis will leave you with much to digest — not just physically, but mentally too, as you leave trying to understand how it is possible to bring out so much flavour from the humblest of ingredients. After all, it's a fish restaurant that's as famous for its fish as for its signature salad, an inspired blend of peeled tomatoes, rocket blossoms, lettuce hearts, radish, chillies and more. Their fish is grilled without seasoning or marinating, but the enormous, custom-built grill in the kitchen allows the juices to fall on the ceramic and cast-iron to return as smoke, which infuses every piece with a remarkable complexity and richness.

How can food so powerful be so simple? Like all great artists, the Dourabeis family operation makes everything look so easy. Yet, since 1932, three generations have toiled to gain expertise in sourcing the finest fish and developing techniques that ensure you will struggle to find fish as flavoursome anywhere in Greece — or the rest of the world, for that matter.

The perfect summer evening begins with dinner at Dourabeis, followed by a stroll along the coastline towards the glittering Mikrolimano, Marina Zea and the rocky outcrops and ancient harbours of Peiraiki, to watch the big boats going in and out of Piraeus port.

 **DOURABEIS**
AKTI DILAVERI 29
PIRAEUS, 185 33

DAILY: 10am – 2am   +30 210 4122092

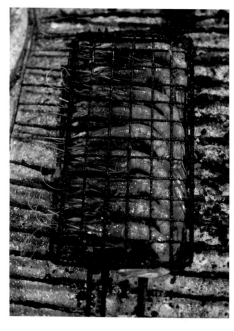

- NIKOS VATOPOULOS -

WRITER AND URBAN EXPLORER

Tell us about your relationship with Athens

I was born in 1960 in Kypseli, an old middle class neighbourhood. I was brought up with the stories of Athens in a way that shaped my imagination and my feeling towards the city. I have been walking in Athens since I was very young, just for the enjoyment of it. Sometimes I wonder if I'm a flâneur, or if I'm just a curious man walking around the city.

You often talk about how modern Athens is a misunderstood city

Visitors don't really take into account that Athens is a new city. There are the ancient ruins, of course, but 150 years ago Athens was a compact, relatively small city by European standards. You could say that Athens is the Brasilia of the 19th century: a city laid out by planners in the 1830s as a new, modern capital city for a new nation.

What interests you most about the city today?

Walking from one end of a typical street to the other, you might come across bauhaus, art deco, modernist, neoclassical and contemporary architecture, as well as the odd ancient ruin, which pop up in the most unexpected places.

What do you most like to share with visitors?

I take my friends to see the ancient hills, which aren't so well known. The Acropolis is one of the ancient hills, of course, but there's also Filopappou, the Phnyx, and the Hill of the Nymphs. It's so poetic. There you can realise what made classical Athens great. You see the landscape, the views to the sea and to the mountains, and you realise what Athens was in history — and nowadays as well.

I think one of the characteristics of Athenian life is the co-existence of the old order with a new youth culture. The new generation is creating an Athenian civilisation that was practically non-existent when I was young. This makes the city of Athens more interesting, more multi-faceted and more intriguing to realise its many layers.

This interview is an extract from Nikos Vatopoulos: Walking in Athens, in the podcast series *We'll Always Have Athens*. Find it on all podcast platforms for more fascinating stories from the city of Athens. You can read more of Nikos' urban reflections in his book, *Walking in Athens*.

24

CHASE
THE SUN

In Athens you are treated to a spectacular show — daily — if only you can find an elevated point to appreciate it. Thank the remarkable geography: the mountains Hymettus, Parnitha and Penteli ring the city, like cupped hands pouring the metropolis into the blue waters of the Saronic Gulf. Get high enough and you can see ships making their way in and out of Piraeus harbour, the Saronic islands and the Peloponnese on the horizon. Then there are the many hills that dot the city (over ten by my count), with the Acropolis most famous, of course, and Lycabbettus the tallest.

But it's not just what you can see, it's the way the fabled Attica light falls over everything, creating an ever-changing palette of rich reds and oranges with the differing weather conditions each day. Just moving around the city, particularly in its hillier parts, during the golden hour before the sun sets is an absolute joy, as sun breaks through the concrete Rubik's Cube that is Athens, bathing whatever it touches in a magical golden glow.

Head for the rocky Strefi Hill which rises above Exarcheia; the Attican Grove Viewing Point; or the viewing area next to Lycabbetus theatre, where cars burn rubber and blast out Greek pop into the long summer nights. But nothing can compare to the view from the thousand-metre peak of Mount Hymettus. If you have the legs, give yourself between one to two hours before sunset to cycle up through Kesariani forest to the summit. You'll be rewarded with increasingly jaw dropping views at each break in the trees, as you climb steadily up above this majestic city.

ATTICAN GROVE VIEW POINT IPIROU 48 ANO KYPSELI, 114 76	MOUNT LYCABETTUS MONOPATI LYCABETTOU LYCABETTUS, 114 71	MOUNT HYMETTUS PAIANIA, 190 02
Search "Attican Grove Viewing Point" on Google Maps	Search "Old School Cantina Lycabettus" on Google Maps	Search "Evzonas (peak) Mount Hymettus" on Google Maps

PHOTOGRAPHY: MICHAEL ODELBERTH

ATH KIDS

25

DEMAND
PIZZA, POWER, RESPECT

Organised by the internationally known music, film and style collective ATH Kids, Brown Sugar Nights is the best way into a rising scene that is putting Athens on the map across the hip hop world. The motto 'Pizza, Power, Respect' gives a sense of the night's playful and inviting vibe, with the latest bangers on the decks, performances from Athens' biggest names and regular deliveries of pizza to the eager crowd.

With artists rapping in both Greek and English, hip hop in Athens is the fastest route to discover a vibrant, multicultural creative scene that largely flies beneath the radar. If you miss Brown Sugar Nights, alternatives are Hip Hop Tuesdays at Bad Tooth and New Kids on the Block at Block 146, also every Tuesday. Check out these five tracks (and their epic videos) for the perfect soundtrack to your adventures in urban Athens:

1. Whip Game – Kareem Kalokoh (ATH Kids)
2. Aspri Mera – Negros tou Moria
3. Kipseli – Moose ft. Negros tou Moria
4. Oi Geitonies – Mc Yinka
5. Chop Money – Athliens (Kid Young ft. Moose, Negros Tou Moria & Daree)

BROWN SUGAR NIGHTS VARIOUS LOCATIONS	BAD TOOTH KAKOURGODIKIOU 6 PSYRRI, 105 54	BLOCK 146 CHAR. TRIKOUPI 146 NEA ERYTHRAIA, 146 71
Instagram:@brownsugarpizza Check social media for dates	DAILY: 2pm - 3am Hip hop: Tuesday nights	Instagram: @newkiddosontheblock Check social media for dates

26

THE TAVERNA
WHERE THE HENS SING REBETIKO

This decadent, underground haunt evokes the outlaw heritage of rebetiko, Greece's urban folk music. The origins of this one-of-a-kind taverna can be traced back to 1885, when the area was green fields and this spot was an open-air poultry farm. After the farmer began feeding the horse and cart drivers waiting to take produce back to Athens, his offering of snacks and wine developed to a full mezze menu, served from a makeshift shack, before proper premises were built in 1950. But it wasn't until 2011 that the hens, which used to have free roam of the space, were replaced with models.

Today, you can squeeze in amongst other patrons to listen to rebetiko musicians play intimate, unplugged sets every night, feast on homemade specialities such as smoked aubergine and fried chickpeas, and guzzle down fresh wine and spirits from the wooden casks on the wall. In the early hours, when the tsipouro is flowing freely and the old jail ballads come out, it becomes an enchantingly intense experience. During the summer months, Kottaroú decamps to Metaxou for rebetiko in a courtyard.

KOTTAROÚ
AGHIAS SOFIAS 43
KOLONOS, 104 44

METAXOU
PITHODOROU 10
METAXOURGEIO, 104 41

WED–SUN: 8:30pm – 2am
+30 210 512 0682

MON–THU: 6pm – 1am
FRI–SAT: 6pm – 3am
SUN: 1:30pm – Midnight

+30 210 522 9290
Live music: WED–SAT
SUN from 3pm

27

FIND THE
UNDERGROUND ON THE ROOF

BIOS may be one of Athens' most established arts venues but, along with its sister venue Romantso, consistently boasts one of the most alternative, diverse and forward-thinking cultural programmes.

The BIOS rooftop has a spectacular view of the Acropolis and projects old films and animation on to the overlooking wall. So, there'll be more than enough to feed your eyes throughout long summer nights that never seem to end. Downstairs, you'll find a theatre, pop-up restaurant and — still — one of the most beautiful bars in Athens, featuring antique furniture and floor-to-ceiling illuminated vintage advertising.

Run by the same cultural organisation, Romantso, a ten-minute walk down Pireos Avenue, also hosts a retro-computer themed bar, arts events and parties — on the roof in summer and basement in winter.

 BIOS
PIREOS 84
KERAMEIKOS, 104 35

ROMANTSO
ANAXAGORA 3
OMONOIA, 105 52

DAILY: 6pm – 3am

MON–FRI: 9am – 1am
SAT–SUN: 10am – 1am

PHOTOGRAPHY: THALIA GALANOPOULOU (ABOVE), PERIKLES MERAKOS (BELOW)

GETAWAYS

Greece boasts over a thousand islands, with more than 200 inhabited. Each one possesses its own unique magic, so you are spoilt for choice. But if you are looking for sun, sea and stimulation within easy reach of Athens, here are the best beach and island escapes for day trips or overnight stays.

YOUR GUIDE TO
THE GREATEST TRIPS

HYDRA

Leonard Cohen may have helped put it on the map for foreigners, but Hydra has a long history of creativity. Just two hours from Athens, today it is indisputably Greece's art island. Hydra is home to a number of prestigious galleries and the Deste Foundation hosts a yearly artists' residency at its Slaughterhouse Project Space, with Jeff Koons dropping by in 2021. Aside from its elegance, Hydra's ban on cars sets it apart. All transport is by foot, boat or donkey.

EVIA

Evia is joined to the mainland by a small strip of land at Halkida, an hour north of Athens, so we could argue over whether it is technically an island. But the ease of access brings Evia's rugged and unspoilt natural beauty even closer. Evia is for the active. It is a favourite of free campers and hikers who tackle its largest peak, Mount Dirfi, or Mount Ochi, with its mysterious Dragon House.

KEA

While not quite at the level of Hydra, Kea is an increasingly fashionable destination. Like Hydra, here you still see the yachts, but less so the decadent houses. In fact, many of Kea's roads are unpaved, which gives it a much wilder atmosphere. It is also the most accessible Cycladic island from Athens, just an hour's ferry ride from Lavrio.

AGISTRI

Agistri is not quite Athens' closest island. But it's worth staying on board the ferry after Aegina — the first stop from Piraeus — for a few more minutes to be rewarded with the crystal-clear waters of Chalikiada beach. Just a 15-minute walk from Skala port, this cliff-lined jewel is a favourite of the young and free Athenians.

28

ALL ABOARD FOR
THE ORIENT

The magic of Athens emanates from its position as a bridge between East and West. And there's nowhere better to pay tribute to this tradition than aboard a section of the old Orient Express. A locomotive and carriages from the legendary train have been lovingly converted into a restaurant, bar, music venue and theatre called To Treno sto Rouf. As some of the site-specific performances are delivered in English, it offers a route in for outsiders to experience Athens' thriving independent theatre scene. Raucous live music nights draw on sounds and styles from Paris, Constantinople and beyond. There's also a bar wagon and a restaurant wagon, so you can be transported as you drink and dine.

 TO TRENO STO ROUF
LEOFOROS KONSTANTINOUPOLEOS
ROUF, 118 54

DAILY: 8pm – Midnight   +30 210 529 8922   totrenostorouf.gr

29

WHERE THE TABLE
IS ON THE FARM

Green spaces are few and far between in the concrete jungle of central Athens, but less than an hour's drive away, Margi Farm is a welcome reminder of rural bliss. Surrounded by vineyards and olive trees, it's set up to showcase a traditional Greek farm and the natural stewardship and agricultural expertise which supports Athens' lively gastronomic scene. Food grown here supplies the historic Margi Hotel in Vouliagmeni, too.

From herbs to vegetables, olive trees, (remarkably sociable) goats and chickens, everything is organic and what's ready for you to harvest during the private dining experiences changes from week to week. Pick up the eggs and veggies for your meal and have a seasonal farm-to-fork menu prepared for you in the outdoor kitchen by a chef. Wash it all down with tsipouro, a spirit distilled from the grapes grown on site. After you've had your fill of food, wine and farm life, head over to Cape Sounion nearby, to watch the sunset over the ancient Poseidon's Temple.

 MARGI FARM
THORIKOU
SARONIKOS, 190 10

Experiences by arrangement.
Book at: info@ourfarm.gr or +30 210 9670924

30

THE CLUB WHERE IT'S
1986 EVERY NIGHT

The best nights are those you never want to end. And at the legendary Athens nightclub Rebound, one night began some time in 1986 and has been going strong ever since. The decor remains unchanged and so does the music: a dark new wave electronic sounds flushed with eighties indie classics and rare euro synth pop set that's forever frozen in time. It's a winning formula that has stood the test of decades. The only thing that changes is a crowd of the beautiful and the damned, who never seem to get any older. Rebound has become something of a hallowed space among artists, with half-Greek American musician Eleanor Friedberger releasing an entire album in 2018 in tribute to her beloved "80s goth disco."

 REBOUND
MITHIMNIS 43
PLATEIA AMERIKIS, 112 52

SAT: midnight – 7am

31

A HAMBURGER HIDEOUT

It's hard to believe this clandestine eatery exists: hidden away in the environs of Syntagma Square, the beating heart of Athens, no less. There is no name, no signage, nothing on the buzzer or on the buttons in the lift. That's why this place has kept its secret for the past 42 years.

But if you manage to set foot inside, you will be rewarded with a spectacular panoramic view of the city that takes in Mount Lycabettus, the Hellenic Parliament, Mount Hymettus, the Saronic Gulf and the Peloponnese – all while you enjoy a simple but delicious menu of *biftekia* (hamburgers), omelettes, salad and fries.

You should look out for a nondescript entrance between a pharmacy and a currency exchange. Head into the corridor, get in the lift and go straight to the top floor. When the doors open, you will need a minute to take it all in...

 HINT: WALK AROUND THE EDGE OF SYNTAGMA SQUARE AND LOOK OUT FOR THE IMAGE CLUES

MON–FRI: 9am – 5pm

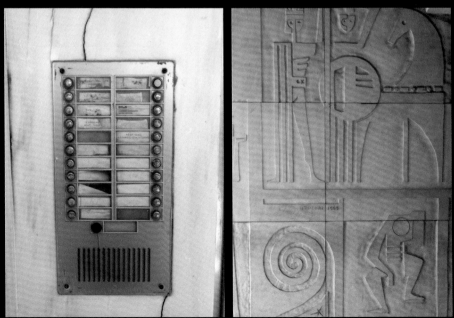

MANY THANKS TO

Everyone who has helped me discover Athens and shared their thoughts or expertise to get this book finished. But especially:

Gareth Jones for opening all the rabbit holes.
Angelos Giotopoulos for (repeatedly) getting me out of trouble.
Theo McInnes for endless tips, editing help and inspiration.
Natassa Pappa for her design wizardry and encouragement.
Iliana Gioulatou for the expert research assistance.
Rachel Howard for all the opportunities she's sent my way (including this book)
Noni Nezi for her stunning illustrations and putting up with my 'process.'
Nena Dimitriou and all the team at **Greece Is** for all of the adventures and insider knowledge.
Penelope Thomaidi for all her advice and energy to explore Greece
Alexia Stamatelatou for bringing me here in the first place.
Thomas Jonglez and Fany Péchiodat for letting me be a part of this amazing series.
All the photographers whose work makes this book shine.
And, finally, my parents, **Ray and Maggie**, for getting me hooked on this expensive drug they call 'travel.'

This book was created by:
Alex King, author and creative direction
Noni Nezi, illustrator
Natassa Pappa & Alex King, graphic design
Theo McInnes, photo editing
Ray and Maggie King, proofreading
Kimberly Bess, additional proofreading

You can write to us at contact@soul-of-cities.com
Follow us on Instagram on @soul_of_guides

Interview extract from 'Nikos Vatopoulos: Walking in Athens'
from We'll Always Have Athens, a podcast by This Is Athens,
the official visitor's guide to the city. Produced by The Greek
Podcast Project.

All photos by Alex King unless credited otherwise

© JONGLEZ 2021
Registration of copyright: May 2021 - Edition: 01
ISBN: 978-2-36195-435-2
Printed in Slovakia by Polygraf